Motherhood
is not for Wimps

Written and compiled by
Catherine & Tim Burr and Beverly & Martin Hopper

Published by
Walrus Productions

Revised edition copyright 1997

Copyright © 1996 by Walrus Productions

Published by Walrus Productions
4805 NE 106th St, Seattle, Washington, 98125
FAX: 206-362-2834
Cover illustration by Kathleen Russell
Typography by Steve Norman of The Durland Group

Printed by Vaughan Printing, Nashville, Tennessee

Burr, Catherine
    Motherhood is not for Wimps / Catherine Burr, -- 1st ed.
    p. cm.
    ISBN 0-9635176-7-8

    1. Quotations. 2. American wit and humor.
I. Title.

Printed in the United States of America
10 9 8 7 6 5 4

We dedicate this book to our children.

Emily & Neil Hopper
Tim & Daniel Burr

Raising Kids
is like buying a book…
one chapter at a time.

The fun never stops…
and the learning never ends.

<u>Question</u>:
How many kids
does it take to drive you crazy?
<u>Answer</u>:
As many as you have.

To handle yourself,
use your head.
To handle your children,
use your heart.

In the family...
it's not who wears the pants
but who changes the dirty diapers.

Have you ever wondered why
newborns don't come with directions?

Four most important attributes
for raising children:
<u>Patience</u>, <u>Love</u>, <u>Consistency</u>
and a sense of <u>Humor</u>.

Babies are such a nice way
to start people.

A baby's laugh is a cure for stress.

A Mother's kiss
soothes all boo-boos & owies.

Just when you think
you've got a stage figured out,
the child moves onto the next stage.

<u>Two stages for parents</u>:

When children ask all the questions
and when
they think they know all the answers.

A child's bedtime
is usually determined
by how tired the parents are.

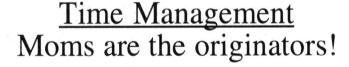

<u>Time Management</u>
Moms are the originators!

Shouldn't Mother's Day
be moved to the first day of school?

Children may know the rules…
parents know the exceptions.

Sweaters are what Mothers put on kids
when Mothers are cold.

The day your child gets the first tooth
can be a painful day for your finger.

As a parent, the only nude scene
you have time for
is chasing a naked toddler.

Screaming kids
make excellent birth control.

And you thought your nights of
being up all night were over.

<u>Bravery:</u>
Taking a toddler on an airplane.
(Keep the peace, pass out ear plugs)

A box of diapers should be
included as carry-on luggage.

Bring extra clothes (for yourself).

New parents are easily identified
by spit-up on their shirts.

Is the phrase "smells like a baby"
really a compliment?

<u>Babies</u>:
How can something so little
require so much equipment?

There is no such thing
as having too many clean diapers.

The finger test
is like playing diaper roulette…
you don't know if it's loaded.

A smart diaper changing accessory
for baby boys is goggles.

Never own just one pacifier.

Battery operated toys
should be outlawed.

Best way to find a lost toy…
go barefoot.

Never walk barefoot
if your daughter plays jacks.

Why do babies wait until you
fall asleep before they cry?

"Sleeps like a baby"
really means awake all night.

Most kids wonder why
"the birds and the bees"
have <u>nothing to do</u> with
the birds and the bees.

Prevent teen pregnancy...
show them stretch marks.

Motherhood adds another
dimension to life…
usually including 10 or 15 pounds.

Teach your children about heaven…
buy a gold fish.

The refrigerator
<u>is</u> the family art gallery.

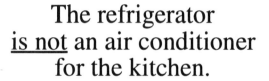

The refrigerator
<u>is not</u> an air conditioner
for the kitchen.

The definition of a toddler: Mini-bulldozer

Beware of toddlers
planning their escape route.

The hardest thing for little boys
... is to sit still.

How do toddlers move so fast
with such short legs?

Kids who run naked down the street
are usually extremely modest
the following year.

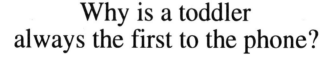

Why is a toddler
always the first to the phone?

You know you've got an active child
if you're on a first name basis
at the local emergency room.

You can expect illness in a family
to follow the domino effect.

Size means nothing…
sometimes it takes two big adults
to give one small child medicine.

If you've never been hated
by your child,
you have never been a parent.

Would *you* really want to have
your temperature taken rectally?

You can always tell
if a couple doesn't have kids
by their white furniture & carpets.

How come muddy feet
always find their way to a clean floor?

Be nervous
when your child walks by
with a stack of towels.

The bathtub: A toddler's lake.

Toddlers who don't want to take a bath will often play in the toilet.

Children are predictable…
except you never know how far
they'll drive you up the wall.

Let animals run wild
…not children.

Diplomacy is the art
of letting your kids get your way.

You can count on others
to raise your children,
but it's better to use your own
fingers and toes.

The warmth of your home
does not depend on your heating bill.

A child may not inherit his
parents' talents, but
he will absorb their values.

Have a peaceful summer… send your kids to camp.

Kids are never fully dressed until they wear a smile.

Have a clean house…
send the kids next door.

Kids come in handy for
teaching parents how to use a computer.

Sometimes it seems
your kids know everything.
(except how to make a living)

Do you consider your kids
profit or overhead?

The people hardest to convince
they're at the retirement age
are children at bedtime.

Why do kids ask "why?"
even after you've told them?

Kids have perfect hearing
only when you
don't want them listening.

It's a bad parenting day when
your child tells you
it's *almost* impossible
to flush a grapefruit down the toilet.

Kids drive us crazy
but we love them anyway.

Children need love…
especially when they don't deserve it.

There is no such thing
as a problem child…
just a child with a problem.

Never forget the
Kindergarten Principle:
KEEP IT FUN!

The world's most important job
is raising another human being.

"They grow up too soon"
is only said by
parents of kids who have.

With your children...
spend half as much money
and twice as much time.

The difference between
ordinary & extraordinary parents
is just that little *extra*.

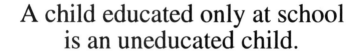

A child educated only at school
is an uneducated child.

All children are born
with a hearing problem...
they can hear everyone
but their mothers.

"Peace & Quiet" usually means the kids are up to something.

Why is it kids always yell "Mom" just when you go to the opposite end of the house?

Want your kids to hear you?
Buy a megaphone!

The modern child
will answer you back
before you've said anything.

When your children are young,
you tend to wish you could have some
of the naps you refused to take as a kid.

The challenge to having leisure time
is keeping your children
from using all of it.

Sleep-overs
(The longest nights of a parent's life)

JACKPOT!
When your kids stay at
a friend's house for the night.

The quickest way to get your kid
to stop playing loud music
is to say you like it.

Give yourself a gift…
buy your teen headphones.

If you really don't like someone
…give their kid a drum.

Kids' memories
improve dramatically
when it's time for their allowance.

Give your kids an allowance
so they'll have money
you can borrow.

<u>Mom's car</u>:
A second home

<u>The Mall</u>:
A teen's home away from home

<u>Credit cards</u>:
A teenage pacifier

Fund your retirement plan… install a pay phone.

<u>Chores</u>:
Give your kids a choice
…do them or else.

Spoiled kids soon become real stinkers.

Don't make it hard for your kids
by making it soft for them.

If you want your children
to keep their feet on the ground,
put some responsibility
on their shoulders.

<u>A Baby</u>:
Turns your life upside-down,
but makes you feel right-side up.

A mother holds a child's
hands for a while…
their hearts forever.

Mom's understand their babies
when no one else can.

Success is getting what you want.
Happiness is wanting what you get.

Every mom has dreams for her kids,
but it is a wise mom who lets
her kids find their own.

How is it that a woman
can carry a baby, a purse,
a diaper bag, groceries
and still unlock the front door?

"Quality time"
is what it's called
when there isn't time for
"Quantity time"

Think of gray hair as military stripes
...you've earned 'em.

Give yourself freedom…
teach your kids
to do laundry.

It is better to build children
than to repair men.

Don't just spend time
with your children…
invest it!

Courage
(Letting your teen have a party)

The number of kids at a party
is in direct proportion
to the size of the aspirin bottle needed.

Teens never read birthday cards;
they just look to see how much
cash is inside.

Why is it that little kids
always play more with the box
than the gift?

Kids' birthday parties:
2 days to plan
2 hours to do
2 weeks to recover from

There's nothing sweeter
than the pitter-patter of little feet
...going to bed.

Don't waste fresh tears over old grief;
you may need those tears tomorrow.

It isn't the mountain
that wears you out,
it's the grain of sand in your shoe.

The two things children wear out
are clothes and parents.

Isn't it exciting
when your child first talks?
Now how do you get them to stop?

You can finally relax
when your kids have done
everything you were afraid of
…and survived.

There's always
room for improvement…
it's the biggest room in the house.

Anger is one letter short of danger.

Count down before blasting off.

Your happiness is a choice
…not a response.

Children need
more models than critics.

Believe in your children.
(If you don't, who will?)

A suspicious parent
makes a devious child.

Teach your children
to have a backbone not a wishbone.

Wouldn't it be nice
if life's problems could hit at sixteen
...when we know everything?

Adolescence is nature's way
of preparing parents
to welcome the empty nest.

Adolescence is not as much a period
as it is an exclamation point!

Teenagers are defined
by physical changes that include
the brain disconnecting from reason.

Kids are like buttons
…always popping off.

It's a bad parenting day
when your child tells the policeman
how fast you were really going.

A joy ride is going anywhere
without the kids.

Try telling your toddler,
"It's not nice to throw your bottle
out of a fast moving car."

If your children offer to water
the house plants, make sure they don't
use the garden hose.

A child who pulls a cat's tail
learns something they can learn
in no other way.

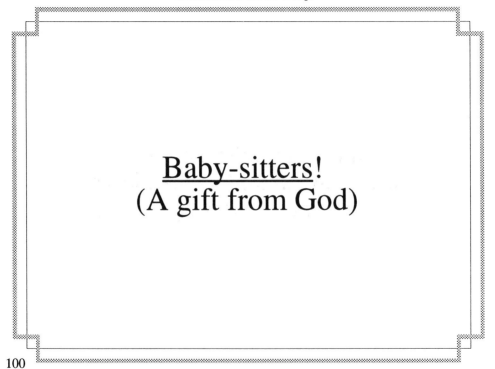

<u>Baby-sitters</u>!
(A gift from God)

The difficulty in finding a baby-sitter
will be in direct proportion
to how desperately you need one.

Entering a teenager's room
is not for the weak of heart.

Don't aggravate yourself;
keep your kid's door shut.

Parents who are afraid
to put their foot down usually
have children who step on their toes.

Memories of childbirth
fade with time, which assures
the survival of the species.

Children usually remember
it's their turn to bring cupcakes
3 minutes before they leave for school.

Kids who only eat
peanut butter sandwiches
will switch to tuna the day after
you buy a case of peanut butter.

Sugar frosted cereal
is the kid version
of a morning cup of coffee.

<u>Beware</u>!
Kids high on sugar

Never ask your kids for the truth
if you don't want to hear it.

It's a bad parenting day when
your child tells your best friend
what you really said.

Children are capable of getting mud
in places you didn't think possible.

Toddlers feel it's their duty
to find out just how much is on
the toilet paper roll.

Buy the toilet paper…
before you run out.

There is nothing more elusive
than the baby's mouth
you are trying to feed.

It's amazing how accurate
a baby's aim is while throwing food.

Save time with toddlers...
put the food directly on the floor.

A good family wallpaper pattern
would be *splatter*.

How come it takes you hours to clean
but kids can make a mess in minutes?

Kids always spill something
extra sticky
on a freshly washed floor.

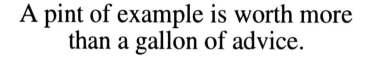

A pint of example is worth more
than a gallon of advice.

No mother can be a great parent
without genuine joy
in the successes of others.

Be patient with your kids' faults
and they will be patient with yours.

Never look down on children
unless you are helping them up.

The best way to bring up a child
is to not let them down.

Children are like wet cement;
whatever falls on them
leaves an impression.

To be a good parent
you need to set down rules.
To be a great parent be consistent
in following through.

One of the first things
an inquisitive child learns
is how little adults know.

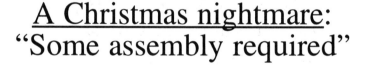

A Christmas nightmare:
"Some assembly required"

Chances are the one toy
your kid wants for Christmas
is the one sold out by October.

Santa really would appreciate it
if your children used the restroom
before they sat on his knee.

<u>Summer</u>:
A mother's nightmare

<u>Back to school</u>:
A kid's nightmare

<u>High School graduation</u>:
A parent's parole

<u>College:</u>
The high cost
of peace & quiet

Do teens have growing pains
or are they *growing pains*?

When the growing gets tough
the tough go to reform school.

Go to group therapy…
Join the PTA.

What is it with teenagers
anyway???

Relax, it's normal for teens
to either sleep, eat or be on the phone
24 hours a day.

Save your kids therapy later…
<u>Apologize now</u>!!!

As we get older, it's amazing
how wise *our own* parents become.

There's nothing wrong
with the younger generation
that twenty years won't cure.

<u>Dinner hour</u>:
Also known as soccer practice.

Be honest about sports…
winning is everything.

Your kid finally scores a goal…
too bad it's for the other team.

The ultimate in youth competition:
<u>A Little League Parent</u>.

The bigger your car
the more kids you can haul…
good reason for a motorcycle.

<u>Mom</u>:
Another word for chauffeur.

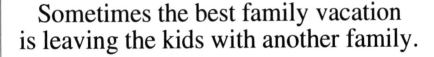

Sometimes the best family vacation
is leaving the kids with another family.

From the time they first walk,
children love to pull on a mother's purse.
Carry a wallet!

Just when you're ready
to throw in the towel…
you discover the washer is full.

<u>All</u> Mothers
are working Mothers.

What job
do you think is harder
than raising kids?

"Being Grounded"
1. Good news when you're an adult.
2. Bad news when you're a kid.

If you want to keep kids at home,
make the atmosphere pleasant
and let the air out of the tires.

One of the chief pleasures
of womanhood, is looking back
at all the men you didn't marry.

By the time
our children have made it
…we've had it.

Every mother has 20/20 hindsight.

A man's work is from sun to sun,
but a Mother's work is never done.

You really feel old when
the kids start reminiscing about
the good old days.

Simply *having* children
does <u>not make</u> mothers.

Those who consider
parenting beneath them
will be above doing it well.

The best way to cheer yourself up
is to cheer your children up.

Hug your kids at home.
Belt them in the car.

A precious gift to your child
...is a listening ear.

Children are not possessions...
they are *on-loan*.

Your children need your presence
more than your presents.

The hardest part of raising children
is learning to let go.

The best Mothers not only
give us life…
but also teach us how to live.

Many a child is kept straight
because the mother bent her knees.

If you don't lie down,
your kids can't walk on you.

Money isn't everything,
but it sure keeps you
in touch with your kids.

Live as you wish
your kids would.

The ultimate pay back:
"Grandparenthood"